RUBY

Beginner's Crash Course—Ruby for Beginner's Guide to Ruby Programming, Ruby On Rails & Rails Programming

Table of Contents

Introduction

Ruby is a computer programming language that was created in the 1990's by a Japanese programmer named Matz whose full name is Yukihiro Matsumoto. It was designed to make programming fun and it is one of the few computer languages that highlights the need for software to be primarily understood by human beings, before a computer understands it.

Ruby is fast becoming one of the most popular languages to use for developing web applications. Ruby on Rails, developed by David Heinemeier Hansson to work with Ruby, is what introduced more people to using Ruby, a language that may otherwise have remained hidden and unheard of by the masses and the result of that is a buzzing community of programmers that welcome beginners and are focused on one thing – producing the highest of quality code.

Many people perceive computer programming as difficult but it really isn't. It does require you to have a certain mindset though, a real thirst for knowledge and learning and, when you adopt this mindset, you will find that programming is not as frustrating as you think it is. It can be fun and successful programming is very rewarding, provided you possess enough patience to see you through.

I have written this book to give inexperienced people an overview of Ruby and Ruby on Rails. Applying the principles and the knowledge that you learn in this book will help you to build up a strong basis in Ruby programming, enough to allow you to move on to more advanced programming.

Chapter 1:
What is Ruby?

Ruby stands alone as the most unique of the object-oriented computer scripting languages. In many other languages, not everything is an object – in Ruby, the opposite is true; absolutely everything is an object. For those who don't know what an object is, think of it as similar to building a car – you have a blueprint that gives you an end product and if you follow it correctly, the object is the end product.

When Matz designed Ruby, it was done in such a way that it was easy for beginners yet powerful enough for the more advanced programmers. This is possible because of the object-oriented nature of the language and because of the addition of carefully selected features from other languages.

Features

- Ruby is not like other object oriented programming languages like C++ or Java, wherein not all things are objects. In C++ and Java, we need to create a class in order to create an object.

- Ruby is one of the popular dynamic programming languages. There are two classes of programming languages in general, namely: a) Static programming languages and b) Dynamic programming languages. Let us see how a dynamic programming language differs from static programming languages.

  Generally, the notions of 'run time' and 'compile time' are often seen in programming languages. When a program is written using a high level programming language, it needs to be translated into the machine code (binary code), before it can be executed. This translation of high level code into machine code is called as 'compilation' and the duration of the process is called as 'compile time'. After getting compiled, the programs become executable, letting the users run them in the form of applications. This running of applications is referred to as 'run time'. During runtime, a dynamic programming language like Ruby exhibits several programming behaviors, which the static programming languages exhibit only during the compile time.

- Ruby is popularly used in the World Wide Web for creating web applications. It has a vast collection of libraries like the "Rails', making it an ideal programming choice for web developers. A popular web application framework, 'Ruby on Rails' has been programmed using Ruby. This framework is popularly used by web developers to build web applications.

- Ruby is also a scripting language. Web developers use scripting languages to control programs written in other languages. They do so by embedding the 'scripts' written in the scripting language, into the program. Similarly, Ruby as a scripting language has been used in the Google Sketchup, a program that accepts 2D picture and converts them into 3D models. The Application Program Interface (API) of Google Sketchup has been written using Ruby; the interface has been embedded into the program so that it controls the generated 3D models. Ruby may not be the easiest of scripting languages that can be used for embedding, but it still holds prominence as a proper scripting language for the completeness of its features.

- Ruby can be downloaded free of cost. There are no trial versions; the complete version of the software can be downloaded freely and can be used for personal or commercial purposes. Its official interpreter is available for free and so are several of its other interpreters that are used for different platforms. Most importantly, it is a free software whose source code can be viewed, modified and used by anyone who wishes to tailor the software according to their own requirements.

Implementations

Official Ruby interpreter

The Matz's Ruby Interpreter (MRI) was Ruby's official interpreter till the version 1.8.The now-retired interpreter was written in C and employed a virtual machine specific to Ruby.

From the version 1.9, YARV or 'Yet Another Ruby VM' has replaced MRI as the official interpreter of Ruby. This implementation is faster than the previous MRI version of interpreters whose virtual machines were slower.

YARV is a virtual machine written in C language and comprises of the following components:

- A Stack Pointer(SP)

- A Program Counter(PC)

- Frame Pointers(FP)

YARV works by compiling Ruby code into an intermediate instruction set. This instruction set is specific to Ruby and is seen in no other programming languages. YARV draws in so many elements of old-ruby like the Ruby parser, garbage collection, the technique of object management etc., It is because YARV is nothing but a module that has been introduced as an extension for old ruby.

Rubinius and JRuby

There are other implementations of the Ruby interpreter namely Rubinius, JRuby, MacRuby, IronRuby eyc., But the most popular alternate implementations of Ruby are Rubinius and JRuby, which can be described as follows:

Rubinius: It is a C++ implementation which currently aims at Ruby 2.1.Some part of the implementation was also written in Ruby. It is a byte code compiler that can perform compilation over the machine code during runtime. It employs the LLVM (Low Level Virtual Machine) for compiling the machine code during runtime.

JRuby: This Java implementation employs the Java Virtual Machine or JVM and currently aims at Ruby 2.2.

Ruby- an inside look

What is a virtual machine

We have seen that different implementations of Ruby have used different kinds of virtual machines. Let us see in detail what a virtual machine is. A virtual machine forms the key portion of a typical Ruby interpreter. Simply put, a virtual machine is basically a software that can be thought of as a virtual computer which works by following a set of predetermined commands.

In general, a typical computer uses and executes 'assembly language' commands for performing a specific task. These assembly language commands are translated into machine code (binary code), the only type of code a computer understands. A similar kind of behavior is emulated by the virtual machine, except that people who write the virtual machine software predetermines what kind of commands the machine can understand. These commands that are predetermined by programmers are called as instructions.

It is not possible to derive these instructions from any other thing, as they are fundamental in nature. The Java Virtual Machine or the JVM uses different instructions for performing different tasks like addition, type conversion and memory storage. Putting together such fundamental instructions results in the generation of the 'bytecode', a code that is run by the virtual machine.

Now, let's see how a virtual machine works with the Ruby code. A Ruby program is saved using the .rb extension. For example, when we save a Ruby program with the name 'ruby_sampl.rb', it is not executed immediately. Firstly, the program undergoes conversion into the byte code, which in turn undergoes interpretation.

You may wonder why the virtual machine is needed for the running of the Ruby code. Why isn't there a 'direct way' for the execution of the Ruby programs, without going through all of these byte code conversions?

Firstly, the byte code is a relatively smaller instruction set when compared to the actual ruby instructions. Obviously, working with a smaller instruction set is simpler and easier, and also results in code optimization.

Secondly, the main advantage of generating a byte code is that, it is platform independent, which means it works on all platforms irrespective of the operating system or the hardware. It means Ruby can be run anywhere by implementing the virtual machine. Java Virtual Machine is by far the most popular virtual machine, employed by several other languages besides Java, like JRuby, Scala, Jython etc.,This was made possible because of the portable nature of the Java Virtual Machine.

The Ruby Virtual Machine

Ruby kept on undergoing changes since its release, when it comes to employing virtual machines. The YARV had to be made the official interpreter of Ruby since the 1.9 version, as the virtual machine of the old-ruby faced problems with optimization. Ruby which was once thought be a very slow language, began slowly improving its performance with every version.

Let us see how a Ruby code is converted into byte code. The working of a compiler or an interpreter can be very interesting to learn, but gets quite theoretical as we delve deep into the details. Still, let us see what happens internally by keeping the rigor to a minimum. The conversion of the ruby code into byte code takes place in two parts as follows:

Tokenizer

A Ruby interpreter like the MRI scans the Ruby code and converts it into small individual units. These individual units are called as 'tokens' and the process is called 'tokenization'. Tokenization is carried out by a program called 'lexer'. For instance, let us take a look at a simple line of arithmetic code (without quotes) as follows:

2+ (6 / 3)-(5)

The above line of code is converted by the lexer into individual units as follows:

NUMBER OPERATOR OPENPAREN NUMBER OPERATOR
NUMBER CLOSEPAREN OPERATOR OPENPAREN
NUMBER CLOSEPAREN

From the above line, we can see that there is a complete shift of focus after the conversion. The lexer has taken a group of characters (numbers in this case) and symbols as input and converted it into a group of units which tell what 'kind of input' was being handled. Both 2 and 200 are evaluated as a NUMBER by the lexer, so the main aim of the lexer is to give a general structure to a line of code. Now, let us see what happens to the tokens given out by the lexer.

Parsing

The tokens given out by the lexer undergo a process called 'parsing' during which the tokens are converted into byte code. The process of parsing is carried out by a program called 'parser'.

Let us continue with the tokens obtained in the last phase as an example:

NUMBER OPERATOR OPENPAREN NUMBER OPERATOR
NUMBER CLOSEPAREN OPERATOR OPENPAREN
NUMBER CLOSEPAREN

From the above set of tokens, the parser looks for certain patterns specifically and identifies a pattern 'NUMBER OPERATOR NUMBER', before converting it into its corresponding bytecode. Similarly, it identifies other patterns too, like 'OPENPAREN NUMBER CLOSEPAREN' and converts them into their associated byte code. The resulting byte code is put together and run on the virtual machine.

A typical ruby interpreter carries out the above two stages in a fairly similar manner, wherein the tokens obtained are looked up for certain patterns specifically and the identified patterns are converted into their corresponding byte code.

However, the two phases are not as simple as portrayed in the example; they are much more complicated. The processes of lexing and parsing involve complex constructs like the AST trees, but only a simple example was provided to you to give you a basic idea of how lexers and parsers work.

You might be thinking that a Ruby code always undergoes interpretation after reading all about how the Ruby interpreters work. But, the two popular Ruby implementations, JRuby and Rubinius employ a compiler just like the static programming languages like C.

What happens in these cases is that, the Ruby code is first compiled into bytecode, before getting executed. Let us see how both Rubinius and JRuby operate on the Ruby code.

Rubinius

Rubinius compiles and executes the Ruby code in two steps:

1. In the first step, the Ruby code is compiled by the Rubinius compiler into Rubinius bytecode.

2. The next step takes place on the Rubinius virtual machine (written using C++ and ruby). In this step, the Rubinius bytecode obtained from the previous step is compiled into the machine code, by the rubinius JIT (Just IN Time) compiler.

The two steps can be illustrated using the following diagram:

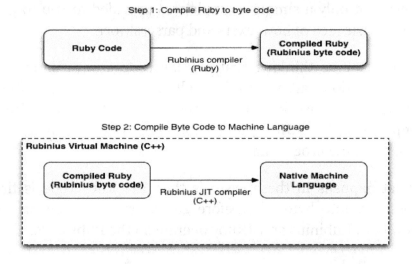

Step 1: Compile Ruby to byte code

Ruby Code → Rubinius compiler (Ruby) → Compiled Ruby (Rubinius byte code)

Step 2: Compile Byte Code to Machine Language

Rubinius Virtual Machine (C++)

Compiled Ruby (Rubinius byte code) → Rubinius JIT compiler (C++) → Native Machine Language

JRuby

Just like Rubinius, Jruby also carries out two steps- one for converting the Ruby code into bytecode, and the other for converting the bytecode into machine code. We can say that these two steps are common to both Rubinius and JRuby; the only difference is that, rubinius uses the Rubinius virtual machine in the second step, where as JRuby uses the Java Virtual Machine for the task.

The following diagram illustrates the two steps that take place when JRuby is used:

Step 1: Compile Ruby to Java byte code

| Ruby Code | → JRuby compiler (Java) → | Compiled Ruby (Java byte code) |

Step 2: Compile Java byte code to machine language

Java Virtual Machine (C)

| Compiled Ruby (Java byte code) | → Java JIT compiler (C) → | Native Machine Language |

The Rubinius bytecode is much simpler and easier to understand when compared to the Java bytecode generated in JRuby, which comes off as complicated and cryptic.

Ruby stands alone as the most unique of the object-oriented computer scripting languages. In many other languages, not everything is an object – in Ruby, the opposite is true; absolutely everything is an object. For those who don't know what an object is, think of it as similar to building a car – you have a blueprint that gives you an end product and if you follow it correctly, the object is the end product.

When Matz designed Ruby, it was done in such a way that it was easy for beginners yet powerful enough for the more advanced programmers. This is possible because of the object-oriented nature of the language and because of the addition of carefully selected features from other languages.

Chapter2:
How to Use Ruby

Ruby is used in many scripting applications like middleware programs, or text processing. It is good for the small tasks and using Ruby to write a program is dead simple – it follows a similar to path to BASIC in writing the type of program that follows a sequence of events.

The expressions in Ruby are top of the class and that helps to make text processing scripts dead easy to write. The syntax is flexible, which stops you from getting bogged down in heavy and cumbersome code. And it is also highly usable for larger systems – Ruby on Rails is a perfect example, containing at least five major subsystems, loads of minor systems and support scripts, libraries and database backends.

What You Need to Help You Learn Ruby

To help you understand and learn Ruby you need to have:

- **An understanding of the concepts of object-oriented programming**

After all, Ruby is all about the object and if you don't have a basic understanding of them, you will struggle to use Ruby for programming.

- **A little knowledge of functional programming**

If you don't have this knowledge, it isn't too much of a problem but it will help you, because Ruby uses blocks quite extensively. You can learn how to create blocks while you are learning to use Ruby but it is helpful to have some prior knowledge.

- **A bit of knowledge about navigation**

The first method of running Ruby scripts is using the command line and knowing how to run scripts, navigate directories and redirect inputs and outputs are essential to learning how to use Ruby to its full extent.

What you Need to Use Ruby

You will need to have the following:

- The Ruby Interpreter

- A text editor – Notepad++ is the best one to use. You can't use WordPad or MS Word, as they are not suited.

- Access to the command line. This will be different depending on which platform you use but the major platforms all have this available without needing you to download any software

Chapter 3:
How To Install Ruby

Windows

To install Ruby on your Windows PC:

- Open http://rubyinstaller.org

- Click on **Downloads**

- Choose the version of Ruby that suits you and click on it, downloading the installer

- Run the installer and follow the on-screen directions. Make sure all boxes are checked if you are only intending to run one version of Ruby, otherwise it will not be available for you to use in the command line and it will not be associated with any .rb or .rbw files

Now you can open your **Start menu** and see what has been added. You should see:

- **Interactive Ruby -** this is nothing more than IRB in the standard command line window

- **RubyGems Document Server -** this will allow the gem server command to be run for the version you downloaded.

- **Start Command Prompt with Ruby -** you can us this to start a command prompt

- **Documentation** - This is the help file format for Ruby API documentation and a PDF version of **The Book of Ruby**

Linux

Ruby is usually installed as standard on Linux distributions but, if you are not sure, you can follow these steps to find out if it is:

- Open a terminal window, sometimes called **shell** or **bash shell**

- Type in and run the command **which ruby**

- If you get a path that says something like */usr/bin/ruby,* it is installed – if you don't get anything like that, it isn't.

- If you want to make sure you have a current version, type in and run the command **ruby –v**

- Compare the number returned to the latest version on https://www.ruby-lang.org/en/downloads/ - at the time of writing, the most up to date stable version is 2.2.2.

If you don't have Ruby installed, use the downloads page to download and install the latest version. Once you have done that, you can install the Ruby packages

- Type in sudo apt-get install ruby1.8 ruby1.8-dev irb rdoc ri

- Open your text editor and input the following information

    o   #!/usr/bin/env ruby

    o   puts "Hello world!"

- Save it as **test rb**

- In your terminal window, change the directory, using the **cd** command, to the one that corresponds to where you saved the test file

- Run the following command – **chmod +x test.rb**

- Next, run this command - **./test.rb** You should now see "Hello World!" displayed on your screen

Ruby is fully installed and ready for use

Chapter 4:
Let's Get Started

It's time to start breaking Ruby down and seeing exactly what she can do and how to do it. I am going to walk you through each element of Ruby, giving code examples, and explain how it all works. So, without further ado, let's get started.

How Your Computer Evaluates Ruby

The Ruby interpreter is the part of the language that makes something out other code you are writing. It reads your code from left to right, top to bottom, that means it starts at the first character of the first line and reads every character in every line, working its way down the code. If there are any errors in your code, the interpreter will stop in its tracks and pop up an error message. That message will normally tell you the line number where the error is.

Ruby Objects

Objects are the heart of Ruby; all data in a Ruby program is manipulated on the single basis that the data is an object. Everything is an object in Ruby – every operation, every variable, every single thing and each object has its own characteristics, which are what makes it different and makes it behave differently from another object.

Ruby Methods

A Ruby method is nothing more complicated than an action that is performed on an object. Ruby contains a number of built in object methods and definitions, one of which is *capitalize*, used for the class strings (more about those later. An example:

- Type in **string1 = "this string is awesome"**

- Now add in the **capitalize method:**

- Type in **string1.capitalise**

- The output would read, **"This string is awesome".**

The **capitalize** method is telling Ruby that the first character of that string should be changed to uppercase.

Something else you may have noticed – the way in which a method is called. The method **string1.capitalize** is broken down as **{{object name}}. {{method name}}**. The object in this example is a string variable and, if you attempted to use the **capitalize** method on an abject that was not a string, you would get nothing more than an error message.

Creating an object for any method is easy:

- def method_name

- #Enter code here

- end

The # is telling the interpreter that the comment is for a human to read and it is to be ignored. The interpreter will ignore any line that begins with a #.

Ruby Classes

A class is simply a blueprint, a set of plans that lets you create objects of a specific type and then to create the methods that relate to them. Classes have something else – a property called "inheritance", which means exactly what you would expect it to mean – a relationship, say grandparents to grandchildren – r that you expect to receive something, or have inherited an attribute from a relative.

In Ruby, those principles are the same, in that it contains parent, children and grandchildren classes. As a rule, a child class will inherit the attributes contained in a parent or grandparent class.

The grandparent class of a Ruby object is called a **superclass** which means, if the object is a string, that object will inherit the properties contained in the string class. That then means that the parent class of **String** is the **String's** superclass.

There is something important that you must not miss here – the superclass of a **string** (a class that informs Ruby how strings are to be treated) is NOT the same as the superclass of a string object. An example of this:

- num1 = "this¬ is a strin¬g"

- "this is a string"

- num1.class

- String

- String.sup¬erclass

- Object

- Object.superclass

- BasicObject

- BasicObjec¬t.supercla¬ss

- nil

All we have done here is set the local variable, **num1,** as a string. When we call out the class of the string, it shows that the class is **String** and, on checking, the superclass is **Object.** The following is an example of what would happen if we used **num1.superclass:**

- num1 = "this¬ is a strin¬g"

- "this is a string"

- num1.super¬class

- #<NoMethodError: undefined method `superclass' for "this is a string":String>

This doesn't work because **num1** is a variable object that inherited the properties from **String** and, because **num1** is not a class it doesn't have any superclass. The following example is an alternative way:

- num1 = "this¬ is a strin¬g"

- "this is a string"

- num1.class

- String

- num1.class¬.superclas¬s

- Object

- num1.class.superclas¬s.supercla¬ss

- BasicObject

- num1.class¬.superclas¬s.superclass.supercl¬ass

- nil

There is a reason why the final value is nil – the **BasicObject** does not have a parent and, as such, doesn't inherit anything, so it can't go any further. What we have done differently here is chained the methods which means that we have carried on applying that method to the statement. And that is one more great thing about Ruby - every time it looks at something and evaluates it, it will return a copy of it and let you carry on evaluating. Take the last line of the above example:

- num1.class¬.superclas¬s.supercla¬ss.supercl¬ass

- nil

What Ruby did was this:

- What is **num1** class? It is a string so Ruby returns **String**

- What is **String** superclass? Because String is a child of the parent class **object,** Ruby returns **Object**

- Because Object is a child of the parent class **BasicObject,** Ruby returns **BasicObject** as the superclass

- Because **BasicObject** is not a child class of anything else, it has no superclass which is why Ruby returns **Nil**

One line, one command. Very simple and very neat. The hierarchy of class inheritance is defined by classes and superclasses so, your next question should be, how do you define and use a class? Here's how:

- class MyClass

- # some code logic

- end

That is all there is to it. **Class** is the opening keyword and that is followed by your class name. Then there is a bit of code and when that's finished, you close it with another keyword, **end.** The keywords **class** and **end** should always be in lowercase – adding capitals will simply result in errors. If you want to use a parent class that you would like this new class to inherit properties from, define it as such:

- class MyChildClass < MyClass

- # some code that is specific to the child class

- end

The < operator is interpreted as meaning that the name of the class on the right is the parent and the left is the child. Also, remember that class names should begin with an uppercase letter and if there is more than one word, you would use CamelCasing – instead of separating the words with a space, hyphen or underscore, you simply join the words together and start each one with a capital, i.e. **CamelCasing.**

Ruby Class Instances

Now you know how to create a class. Now think of a class as a recipe and that contains a list of the ingredients and the instructions for making a particular recipe. Once you make that recipe, let's say chocolate muffins, for example, each muffin becomes an instance of the class. You create an instance like this:

- muffin = ChocolateMuffin.new

Again, that is all there is to it. The only bit of this statement that creates the instance is **ChocolateMuffin.new.** To use an object, it has to be stored somewhere so we use **Muffin**, which is a local variable. By doing this, you can reuse the instance.

Chapter 5:
How Is Data Structured In Ruby?

Data manipulation is the very core of any programming language. In order to help manipulate the data in a structured way, computer scientists came up with something called data structures.

These are containers for specific data types. Words and formulas are handled differently, in the same way that letters and characters are handled in a different way to numbers in most cases.

Variables

Variables are the most basic container for data storage. The names of the variables must be unique to their scope – let's say you want to create a piece of a program that adds up two numbers. You would have to set up one container for each number and then set the function that goes between the two numbers.

The reason for doing it this way is so that the user doesn't have to make any changes to the source code whenever they want to do the calculation. In Ruby programming, each one of these containers is a variable so you would have something like this:

- sum = num1 + num2

Instead of

- sum = 19 + 20

Most computer programming languages contain variables and Ruby is no different. There is a wide range of different ones though so, to avoid any confusion, I am going to go over some of the more common ones:

Local

This variable can only be used in a finite part of the program, like a method or a function. As soon as you come out of that particular part of the program, those variables become obsolete and cannot be used again.

Global

Global variables can be used throughout the whole program and are not restricted to one specific area. This means that, once you have used them in a specific area, they are not destroyed and can be used elsewhere.

Constants

These are classed as "sacred" global variables. The value of such a variable remains constant for the entire life of the program unless you change them. If you do, you will get a warning message because Ruby doesn't like this happening.

Class

Class variables are limited to the class in which they are defined at the start of the variable.

Instance

These variables are limited to just one instance of a class and are defined by the use of an @ at the start of the variable name

How to Use the Different Variable Types

- **Local** – variable name should begin with an underscore or a lowercase letter

- **Global** – variable name should begin with a $

- **Constants** – Variables should begin with an uppercase letter but are normally written entirely in capitals

- **Class** – Tells how long the side of an object is in a class. An example would be **@@length = 10 #**

- **Instance** – Tells how long the side of a specific object is

These rules are not comprehensive and there are words that you simply can't use as variable names. These are known as **reserved** words and they are used by Ruby to identify particular language elements. Those words are:

- _FILE-

- _LINE_

- BEGIN

- END

- alias

- and

- begin

- break

- case

- class

- def

- defined?

- do

- else

- elsif

- end

- ensure

- false

- for

- if

- in

- module

- next

- nil

- not

- or

- redo

- rescue

- retry

- return

- self

- super

- then

- true

- undef

- unless

- until

- when

- while

- yield

Ruby Strings

Strings are sequences of characters, for example, words or a series of words. They are not sentences:

- string1 = 'a'

- string2 = 'This is a string'

There are two things that are happening in the example above – the first one is that we have used local variables and the second is that, to define the variable content, we used single quotes. Although **string1** only contains one letter, it is still classed as a string because we have declared it inside the single quotes.

Ruby knows exactly how to treat a variable because it looks at the way it is declared. You don't have to use single quotes, you can use doubles but, whichever one you choose, you must be consistent throughout. In other words, you cannot start a string with single quotes and end it with doubles or vice versa.

- num1 = 9

The above is another example. **Num1** has been set with a value of 9 so if you were to type in **num1 + 1** you would get a return of **10**. However, if you put single quotes around the 9

- num1 = '9'

That would be telling Ruby that 9 is actually a string and not a number. If you were to type **num1 + 1** it would throw up an error message, something along the lines of =>#. The interpreter is telling you that you have given it both a string and a number and it cannot add them up – it doesn't know how to. If we go a step further and you did this:

- num1 = '9'

- num2 = '1'

- num1 + num2

The result would look like this:

- "91"

The result comes about because Ruby takes both of the strings and it squashes them together. If you specify values in between quotes, you are telling the interpreter that you don't want it to be translated; instead, you want the interpreter to take the content that is between the quotes – the exact content. In this case, the **9** is treated as an ordinary letter, not as a number.

Ruby Collections

So far, we have talked about individual bits of data that can be stored in local variables or created as instances of a class. Bu, what about if you want to use several data pieces at once, a collection like a series of numbers that you perhaps wanted to put in an ascending order or a list of names that you wanted to be sorted into alphabetical order. To allow us to do that, Ruby provides us with two tools to do this with – arrays and hashes.

Arrays

The best way to explain an array is to show you what one would look like:

- Food

- [0] = Chicken

- [1] = Rice

- [2] = Steak

- [3] = Fish

- [4] = Shrimp

- [5] = Beef

Instead of having six separate variables, one for each of the food types, instead we have one array that lists and stores each item inside its own container. The numbers indicate the key of the specific element within the array and you will note that we always start from zero – 0 is the first element, 1 is the second, and so on. To produce this array in Ruby, you would input the following:

- food = ['chicken', 'rice', 'steak', 'fish', 'shrimp', 'beef']

-     ['chicken', 'rice', 'steak', 'fish', 'shrimp', 'beef']

- food.count

-     6

Each element is enclosed in single quotes because what we are doing here is storing strings in the elements. The array class in Ruby has a few methods that can be used straightaway, such as **count -** as used in the example above. What it does s counts the elements that are in the array and returns the value. Even though there are only 5 on the index, the count is 6 – this is because we started at zero.

Now you have created the array, each individual item can be accessed by invoking the specific name of the array, followed up with the index number of the food item:

- food[0]

- "chicken"

- food[1]

- "rice"

- food[2]

- "steak"

- food[6]

- nil

The reason why the return is nil for **food 6** is because there isn't a 6 in the array – or at least nothing stored in it anyway. So Ruby will automatically set the sequence as an ongoing sequence – food [6], food [7], etc. and, to add in another item to the array you would simply set the next element to the value you want it to be:

- food[6] = 'carrots'

- "carrots"

- food

- ["chicken", "rice", "steak", "fish", "shrimp", "beef", "carrots"]

- food.count

- 7

Another way to add elements to the array is to use an operator called **append** - << - all this does is adds something to the end of the array you are adding to. The difference is that you do not need to specify any index positions with this operator; all you need to do is this:

- food << "irish potato"

- ["chicken", "rice", "steak", "fish", "shrimp", "beef", "carrots", "irish potato"]

- food << 42

- ["chicken", "rice", "steak", "fish", "shrimp", "beef", "carrots", "irish potato", 42]

Whatever is added in after << is automatically added on to the end of the array, which is convenient because it means you can add in variables and other objects without needing to worry about the actual content:

- sum = 10 + 23

- 33

- food << sum

  ["chicken", "rice", "steak", "fish", "shrimp", "beef", "carrots", "irish potato", 42, 33]

All we have done is created a local variable that we called **sum** and we then pushed the value to the end of the array. If you want, you can add arrays on to the end of other arrays:

- name_and_age = ["Marc", "Gayle", 28]

- ["Marc", "Gayle", 28]

- food

- ["chicken", "rice", "steak", "fish", "shrimp", "beef", "carrots", "irish potato", 42, 33]

- food.count

- 10

- food << name_and_age

- ["chicken", "rice", "steak", "fish", "shrimp", "beef", "carrots", "irish potato", 42, 33, ["Marc", "Gayle", 28]]

- food.last

- ["Marc", "Gayle", 28]

- food.count

- 11

You will note that, on this example, the final element is an array that contains three elements but, even so, it is still counted as a single element inside the array. The count number has now risen to 11 and if you wanted to know how many elements are inside any specific element of the array, the last element for example, you would do this:

- food.last.count

- 3

There are a couple of other interesting Ruby methods that you can use off the bat, including **first, last, length** and **include** and these would be followed by the object you are checking for, i.e. **empty?, eql?** and **sort.**

- food

- ["chicken", "rice", "steak", "fish", "shrimp", "beef", "carrots"]

- food.first

- "chicken"

- food.last

- "carrots"

- food.length

- 7

- food.count

- 7

- food.include?("chicken")

- true

- food.include?("filet mignon")

- false

- food.empty?

- false

- food[0]

- "chicken"

- food[0].eql?("chicken")

- true

- food[0].eql?("beef")

- false

- food.sort

- ["beef", "carrots", "chicken", "fish", "rice", "shrimp", "steak"]

So, what we've done here is put the string inside double quotes, after the **eql?** And the **sort** method arranges alphabetically and by number, from low to high. Anything can be stored in elements; you don't have to stop at strings. You can mix as well – some elements can have numbers in them and others can have strings. If you wanted an array of numbers, you would do this:

- numbers = [1, 2, 3, 4, 5, 6]

- [1, 2, 3, 4, 5, 6]

Remember that we said earlier indexes must start at zero. In this example, you can see why that is important. To reference the number **1**, the array reference must be **0** because that is the first element of the array

- numbers[0]

- 1

- numbers[1]

-    2

- numbers[6]

-    nil

- numbers.first

- 1

- numbers.last

- 6

- numbers.count

- 6

- numbers.length

- 6

- numbers.include?(3)

- true

- numbers.include?(10)

- false

- numbers.empty?

- false

- numbers[1]

- 2

- numbers[1].eql?(1)

- false

- numbers[1].eql?(2)

- true

We are evaluating numbers so the objects that are contained in the brackets must not be in double quotes otherwise Ruby would not be able to find them – it would be searching for a string instead so be careful how you use those quote marks!

- numbers.include?("3")

  - false

- numbers[1].eql?("2")

  - false

Ruby Iterators

Iterators are Ruby mechanisms that help you to move through data structures that contain multiple elements, and to examine each of the elements. The most commonly used iterator is **each** and this is a method that is contained in the array class and is included in Ruby. Let's say that we wanted to print off a list of all of the items we have stored in the food array:

- o food

- ["chicken", "rice", "steak", "fish", "beef"]

- food.each do |x|

- puts x

- end

- chicken

- rice

- steak

- fish

- beef

There are a couple of things to be aware of:

1. **each** can only be called on data collections

2. Once **each** is called, you must pass a data block to it. A block is nothing more than a piece of contained code and, by passing the block, you are saying that you want the code applied to each of the elements you look at.

Block

You can use a block in two ways – first, like the above example, where you would do this:

- do |variable| #some code end

Blocks must always be used with an iterator. You can define the block without one but to execute that block, you need the iterator. This is why we called **do.x** after **food.each** in an earlier example. Your block can have one or more variables in it but they are local to that specific block only. That means, once you leave the block, they will be destroyed. If you had two blocks, the variable **x** could be used in both and neither would affect the other. Another way to use blocks is:

- food.each { |x| puts x }

Here, the curly brace at the start replaces the variable **do** and the closing brace replaces **end**. If your operation contains just one line this is the most convenient method but it may be a little harder to read the code at a later date – you might find it easier to use **do** and **end**, that's down to your personal preference.

Blocks use variables because the elements in the collection have not been modified, unless you chose to modify them. What happens is this – for every iteration throughout the array, a copy is stored in **x**, which is then used in the block. IF you went through the food array, **x** would look something like this:

First iteration:

- food[0] = 'chicken'

- x = food[0]

- x = 'chicken'

Second iteration:

- food[1] = 'rice'

- x = food[1]

  x = 'rice'

Third iteration:

- food[2] = 'steak'

- x = food[2]

- x = 'steak'

If you used numbers, it would be better illustrated that the values do not change in the original array

- numbers = [1, 2, 3, 4, 5]

  - [1, 2, 3, 4, 5]

- numbers.each do |x|

- ... x = x + 2

- ... puts x

- ... end

- 3

- 4

- 5

- 6

- 7

- numbers

  - [1, 2, 3, 4, 5]

Ruby Hashes

Hashes are simply collection types, of key-value pairs, to be precise. These are a combination of the container name, or key, and the value or contents of the container.

- a => "Marc"

In this example, the name or key is **a** and the value or contents is **Marc**. So, a hash is simply a list of these pairs, each separated by a comma and looking something similar to this:

- a =>"Marc", b => "Cheyenne", c => "Alexander", d=> "Mia"

There are some differences between arrays and hashes though:

1. These keys are not specifically integer keys; they can be integers, characters, strings, or any other object type

2. They are not ordered – Ruby doesn't take nay notice of the order when it is looking in hashes

3. Despite the fact that they are not ordered, if you were to iterate through a hash (I will show you that in a while), Ruby would look at them in the order they were added n to the hash. This is not the same way that array keys are ordered.

There are a lot of different ways to create a hash but the most common ways are something similar to the examples below. To start a hash that is empty or has no values:

- day = Hash.new

- {}

A hash that has values would look something like:

- names = Hash["a" => "Marc", "b" => "Cheyenne", "c" => "Alexander", "d" => "Mia"]

- {"a"=>"Marc", "b"=>"Cheyenne", "c"=>"Alexander", "d"=>"Mia"}

- names2 = {"a" => "Marc", "b" => "Cheyenne"}

- {"a" => "Marc", "b" =>"Cheyenne"}

You do not need to use the keyword **hash** in order to create one, nor do you need to use the square brackets ([]). You can if you wish or you could just use the curly braces. The keys do not need to be enclosed in quote marks either, unless you intend to use the strings as a key. Ruby does require => to be used to assign the value on the right of the => to the key on the left. If, for example, you attempted to put in **names2** without the quotes, you would probably see something like this error message:

- names2 = { a => "Marc", b => "Cheyenne"}

- #<NameError: undefined local variable or method `a' for main:Object>

In order to access the values, you must specify the hash name as well as the key to value you want access to:

- names

- {"a"=>"Marc", "b"=>"Cheyenne", "c"=>"Alexander", "d"=>"Mia"}

- names["a"]

- "Marc"

- names["c"]

- "Alexander"

- names[a]

44

- #<NameError: undefined local variable or method `a' for main:Object>

Because we didn't use the quote marks for **names[a]**, Ruby sees **a** as a method or a local variable and it can't locate a value for it, giving you an error message. If you were to attempt to access what looked like a legitimate value using a legitimate key that has no value assigned to it, you would normally see a return of **nil.**

- day["a"]

- nil

- day[9]

- nil #For you Day9 fans, don't worry... I am a fan too :)

Let's say that you wanted to create hash that has a default value for every value contained in it. You could do this:

- year = Hash.new("2012")

- {}

- year[0]

- "2012"

- year[12]

- "2012"

What we have done so called the method **new** on the class **Hash** and passed a default value of **2012** in to the method. When you try to access a non-existent value, instead of coming back with **nil**, Ruby will now give you the default value that

45

you specified. There are a few different methods that you can use with hashes:

- names.keys

- ["a", "b", "c", "d", "e"]

- names.values

- ["Marc", "Cheyenne", "Alexander", "Mia", "Christopher"]

In this, the **keys** simply return the keys in the hash and **values** will return all the values.

- names.length

- 5

- names.has_key?("a")

- true

- names.has_key?("z")

- false

- ?names.has_key("a")

- #<NoMethodError: undefined method `has_key' for #<Hash:0x55c797d7>>

Did you spot that the **has key** method actually reads **has key?** If you left the ? out, you would see an error like the one in the last row above. All **has key?** does is checks to see if any of the keys in the hash match the values in the brackets – if there is one, **true** will be returned, if not then **false** is returned.

- f_names = names

- {"a"=>"Marc", "b"=>"Cheyenne", "c"=>"Alexander", "d"=>"Mia", "e"=>"Christopher"}

- l_names = {"g" => "Gayle", "h" => "Gayle", "j" => "Jackson", "m" => "Brown"}

- {"g"=>"Gayle", "h"=>"Gayle", "j"=>"Jackson", "m"=>"Brown"}

- f_names.merge(l_names)

- {"a"=>"Marc", "b"=>"Cheyenne", "c"=>"Alexander", "d"=>"Mia", "e"=>"Christopher", "g"=>"Gayle", "h"=>"Gayle","j"=>"Jackson", "m"=>"Brown"}

- f_names

- {"a"=>"Marc", "b"=>"Cheyenne", "c"=>"Alexander", "d"=>"Mia", "e"=>"Christopher"}

- l_names

- {"g"=>"Gayle", "h"=>"Gayle", "j"=>"Jackson", "m"=>"Brown"}

What we have done here is create a new hash called **f names** simply by assigning it to **names**. Then another one called **l names** that has a number of names inside it. We then merged the hashes together to create one hash. However, we only ran **merge**; we didn't actually assign the results to any particular variables and, as such, it wouldn't have been stored. If you look at the values of **1 names** and **f names,** you can see that they are identical to what they were before **merge** was run. If you want to store those values, you would need to do something along the lines of:

- master_hash = f_names.merge(l_names)

- {"a"=>"Marc", "b"=>"Cheyenne", "c"=>"Alexander", "d"=>"Mia", "e"=>"Christopher", "g"=>"Gayle", "h"=>"Gayle", "j"=>"Jackson", "m"=>"Brown"}

Symbols

Symbols are types of object that resemble strings but are not quite strings. The big difference between a symbol and a string is that symbols always start with a colon. Symbols play very nicely with hashes because they can be used as keys in place of strings.

- f_names

- {:a =>"Marc", :b =>"Cheyenne", :c =>"Alexander", :d =>"Mia", :e =>"Christopher"}

- f_names[:a]

- "Marc"

This is a good thing because it means no more worrying about the quotes around the values and the keys but you still know the names for the keys:

- pets = {:dog => "Cookie", :cat => "Snowy", :fish => "Goldie"}

- {:dog=>"Cookie", :cat=>"Snowy", :fish=>"Goldie"}

- pets[:dog]

- "Cookie"

- pets[:fish]

- "Goldie"

Using symbols with hashes is much easier than using strings with keys. Of course, you can use hashes for just about anything else in Ruby since their main function is the storage of values and making it easier for the interpreter to retrieve them

The *BEGIN* Statement

If you want a piece of code to be executed before running the main program, place the code in a BEGIN statement. It's syntax is as follows:

BEGIN {

code

}

The following example illustrates how to use a BEGIN statement.

Example:

#!/usr/bin/ruby

puts "This is the main Program"

BEGIN {

puts "This is executed before the main program"

}

This will produce the following result:

This is executed before the main program

This is the main Program

The *END* Statement

If you want a code to be executed at the end of a program, you can use the 'END' statement for specifying the code.

The syntax for the END statement is simple and is as follows:

END {

block of code

}

The following example not only illustrates the usage of the END statement, but also illustrates the difference between the BEGIN and END statements:

#!/usr/bin/ruby

puts "This is the main Program"

END {

puts "This is executed at the end"

}

BEGIN {

puts "This is executed before the main program"

}

The above code generates the following output:

This is executed before the main program

This is the main Program

This is executed at the end

Comments in Ruby

If you want the ruby interpreter to ignore a statement or several statements or lines of codes, begin the line of statement(s) with a hash(#) character. When you begin a line with a hash character, it is treated as a comment and is skipped by the interpreter. Thus, comments are used to hide lines of the code.

An example of a comment is as follows:

this is a comment. So, it is ignored by the interpreter.

A command can also follow an expression or a statement on the same line. Comments are mainly used for documenting the code.

city= "Dallas" # I am a comment, so I am ignored.

Multiple lines of comments can be specified as follows:

I'm a comment

I'm a comment too.

I'm a comment too.

We are all comments.

If you want to specify several lines of comments as a single block, you can use the =begin/=end statements as follows:

=begin

I'm a comment

I'm a comment too.

I'm a comment too.

We are all comments

=end

Chapter 6:
Input and Output Methods in Ruby

Any data that is fed into a program through a keyboard or another program or a file, is called as an input. The program processes the input and produces another data called as output. The program may send the output to the screen or other programs or files.

Though they may look simple, the topics of input and output in Ruby can get quite big as we proceed through different levels. The following examples illustrate the concepts of inputs and outputs in their most basic forms for a better understanding. There are several methods available in Ruby that can be used for performing the operations of input and output. These methods belong to different classes like IO, File, Kernel, Dir etc;

Reading input from the screen

Now, let us learn through a few examples of how input can be read from the screen.

We can use the variable $stdin for reading input from the screen. The standard input stream is held by $stdin, which is a global variable.

```
#!/usr/bin/ruby

inpt = $stdin.read

puts inpt
```

The above example uses the method 'read' for reading input from the screen.

```
inpt = $stdin.read
```

The read method works by reading the data, until the end of the file is reached. If you are using the Windows operating system, pressing the keys Ctrl+Z produces EOF. If you are using Unix, pressing Ctrl+D will do the job.

```
$ ./readdata.rb
```

Lizzie Luke

Lizzie Luke

When a program devoid of any parameters is launched, data provided by the user is read by the script. It keeps on reading the data, until Ctrl+W or Ctrl+D are pressed.

```
$ echo "Jon" | ./readdata.rb
```

Jon

```
$ ./inputs.rb < Fruits
```

Mango

Apple

Banana

Strawberry

Grape

Orange

Pineapple

Peach

Blueberry

If necessary, we can redirect the script such that it reads data from other files or programs.

The commonly used method for reading data from the screen is the gets method.

```
#!/usr/bin/ruby

print "Enter your city: "

city = gets

puts "You live in #{city}"
```

Let us take a look at the above code step by step:

We have used the gets method for reading the name of the city in which the user lives:

city = gets

Through the above line of code, the city name provided by the user is read by the gets method. The data string provided by the user is assigned to the variable 'city'.

puts "you live in #{city}"

The above line of code prints the data read from the user to the screen. Interpolation can be used such that the string includes the variable.

$ ./readtheline.rb

Enter your city: Dallas

You live in Dallas

Writing output to the screen

There are several methods available in Ruby if you want to print an output on the screen. Of these methods, the print and puts methods of the Kernel module are widely used. Any Ruby object can access these methods from the kernel module.

Take a look at the following example:

#!/usr/bin/ruby--->this is nothing but Ruby's pathname given as a comment

print "Jon "

print "Jasper\n"

puts "Lizzy"

puts "Luke"

In the code given above, both the print and puts statements write the outputs to the screen. The only difference is that, the puts method automatically inserts a newline character at the end, while the print statement doesn't. Simply put, if you want a statement to be printed in a new line, you have to specify the newline character '\n', if you are using the print statement. On the other hand, if you are using the puts statement, you need not specify any such character; it automatically adds the '\n' character at the end. Take a look at the print statements given in the code:

print "Jon "

print "Jasper\n"

In the above case, the print statement prints the first string 'Jon' and then prints the next string 'Jasper' immediately next to Jon, as no new line character is specified between the print statements of 'Jon' and 'Jasper'. Observe that a new line character is specified only after the second statement.

Now, take a look at the second part of the code:

puts "Lizzy"

puts "Luke"

We can see that no new line characters are specified with both the puts statements. Now, save the code with the name 'printoutput.rb', which gives the following output on the screen.

$ ./printoutput.rb

Jon Jasper

Lizzy

Luke

Observe that the strings 'Lizzy' and 'Luke' are printed on different lines, even though no newline character is used.

The print method performs equivalent function as that of the $stdout statement. The standard output stream is held by the global variable $stdout. The following example illustrates the usage of the $stdout variable.

#!/usr/bin/ruby

$stdout.print "I love ice-cream \n"

```
$stdout.puts "I hate mangoes"
```

Thus, the $stdout variable has been used to print two lines in the above example.

There are three other methods available in Ruby, which are used for printing output to the screen. Observe the methods in the following code:

```
#!/usr/bin/ruby

p "Lizzy"

p "Luke"

printf "Lizzy is %d years old\n", 23

putc 'M'

putc 0xA
```

You can see that we have used three methods in the above code namely:

- **p**:

  For every object printed on the screen, the inspect method is called by the 'p' statement, after which a newline follows.

  p "Lizzy"

  p "Luke"

  OUTPUT:

  "Lizzy"

"Luke"

You will clearly understand the p method if you study the output of the following example

```
class Thing

 def inspect

   "Result of inspect"

 end

end

puts Thing.new

p Thing.new
```

The output of the above code is as follows;

#<Thing:0x0000000381d3f8

Result of inspect

If you observe the output, you can see that the result of the inspect method is printed by the p method.

- **printf**:

  Most of you must be familiar with the printf method of C Language. String formatting is allowed by the printf method as is evident from the following line of code and its output:

  printf "Lizzy is %d years old\n", 23

  OUTPUT:

Lizzy is 23 years old.

- **putc:**

The putc method is used for printing a single character onto the screen.

Example:

putc 'M'

OUTPUT:

M

A new line can be printed using the putc method using the hexadecimal code as follows:

putc 0xA

The chomp method

The white spaces which linger at the end of a string can be removed by using a method named 'chomp' method. This method is used while performing input operations. The name of the method and its functionality are taken from Perl. The following two examples illustrate the usage of the chomp method during input operations:

Example 1:

```
#!/usr/bin/ruby

print "Enter any word: "

inpt = gets
```

puts "This word has #{inpt.size} characters"

In the above code, we have accepted a word from user and calculated the number of characters present in the word. The resultant output is as follows:

$ ./nochomp.rb

Enter any word: Lion

This word has 5 characters

You can observe from the above output that the number of characters present in the string 'Lion" is calculated as 5, instead of 4. The reason is that, the new line at the end of the string has also been counted.

If you want the correct string length as the output, the newline character at the end of the string needs to be removed and the chomp method is used for doing the job. Let us rewrite the above program using the chomp method as follows:

#!/usr/bin/ruby

print "Enter any word: "

inpt = gets.chomp

puts "This word has #{inpt.size} characters"

The above code produces the following output:

$ ./chompthestring.rb

Enter any word: Lion

This word has 4 characters

We get the correct number of characters this time, as we have 'chomped off' the newline character at the end using the chomp method.

Chapter 7:
Conditional Structures in Ruby

Just like all the modern programming languages, conditional structures are available in Ruby. Let us take a look at all the conditional statements offered by ruby. You will also learn about the modifiers offered by Ruby.

The *if...else* Statement

The if..else statements are used for executing codes based on conditions. All values are evaluated as true except the *nil* and *false* values, which are evaluated as false.

Note: For the *else* part, Ruby does not use either else if or elif. It uses the reserved word 'elsif'.

The code written in the if-block gets executed if the if-condition evaluates to true. If the if-condition evaluates to false, the code written in the else statement is executed.

A reserved word 'then' separates the if-condition and the block of code. A semicolon or a newline character can also be used to separate the if-statement and the code block.

The Syntax of the if...else statement is as follows:

if conditional [then]

       block of code

[elsif conditional [then]

       block of code

[else

block of code

end

The following example illustrates the usage of the if...else statement:

```ruby
#!/usr/bin/ruby

a=10

if a > 20

    puts "a is greater than 20"

elsif a <= 20 and a!=0

    puts "a is 10"

else

    puts "The number cannot be guessed"

end
```

x is 10

The *if* modifier

The if modifier is used to execute a code if the condition evaluates to true. Take a look at its syntax to get a clear idea of how it should be used:

Syntax:

code if condition

The following example illustrates the usage of the if modifier:

```
#!/usr/bin/ruby
```

```
$a=1
```

```
print "'a' is a character\n" if $a
```

The above code generates the following output:

'a' is a character

The *unless* statement

The unless..else statement is similar to the if...else statement, except that the conditions are evaluated in the opposite manner i.e. if the condition evaluates to false, the code written in the *unless block* is executed. If the condition evaluates to true, the code written in the else block is executed.

The Syntax of the unless...else statement is as follows:

unless conditional [then]

  code

[else

  code]

end

The following Example illustrates the usage of the unless statement:

```
#!/usr/bin/ruby
```

```
a=10
```

```
unless a>20

  puts "a is less than 20"

else

  puts "a is greater than 20"

end
```

The above code generates the following output:

a is less than 20

The *unless* modifier:

The if modifier is used to execute a code if the condition evaluates to false. The Syntax of the unless modifier is similar to that of the if modifier and is given as follows:

code unless conditional

The following example illustrates the difference between the if modifier and the unless modifier

```
#!/usr/bin/ruby

$x = 10

print "1.The value is true \n" if $x

print "2.The value is false\n" unless $x

$x = false

print "3.The value is false\n" unless $x
```

The above code generates the following output:

1.The value is true

3.The value is false

The *case* Statement

The case statement in Ruby is accompanied by one or several 'when' clauses. The case expression is compared with the when expression(s), and if a match is found in a when clause, the code specified in that when clause is executed.

Let's take a look at the syntax of the case statement for a better understanding;

Syntax:

case expression

[when expression [, expression ...] [then]

   code]...

[else

   code]

end

The === operator is used for comparing the expressions of the case statement and the when clause. The expression of the case statement is evaluated as the right operand and the expression of the when clause acts as the left operand. If none of the when clauses match the case expression, the code specified in the else statement is executed.

The reserved keyword 'then' is used to separate the when clause and its associated code. A semicolon or a newline character can also be used to separate the when clause from the block of code.

Consider the following syntax consisting of a case statement, with several when clauses and an else statement at the end:

case expo

when exp1, exp2

  satement1

when exp3, exp4

  satement2

when expr5, expr6

  satement3

else

  satement4

end

The above syntax is similar to the following syntax:

_tmp = expo

if exp1 === _tmp || exp2 === _tmp

  statement1

elsif exp3 === _tmp || exp4 === _tmp

  statement2

```
else
    statement3
end
```

The following example illustrates how a case system is used:

```ruby
#!/usr/bin/ruby

$age =  3
case $age
when 0 .. 2
    puts " It's a toddler"
when 3 .. 6
    puts "It's a little child"
when 7 .. 12
    puts " It's a child"
when 13 .. 18
    puts " It's a youth"
else
    puts " It's an adult"
end
```

The above code generates the following result:

It's a little child

Chapter 8:
Loops in Ruby

Just as in every programming language, you can use loops in Ruby if you want a repeated execution of the same block of code for a required number of times. Ruby supports the following loop statements:

- while

- for

- until

- break

- redo

- retry

The *while* Statement

A while statement is used to execute a block of code repeated number of times, as long as a condition is satisfied. Take a look at its syntax:

while conditional [do]

block of code

end

The while statement executes the *block of code,* as long as the 'conditional' evaluates to true. The reserved word 'do' separates the conditional and the *block of code*. A backslash, semicolon or a newline character can also be used to separate them.

The following example illustrates the use of the while statement:

```
#!/usr/bin/ruby

$j = 1

$n = 5

while $j < $n  do

   puts("This is the statement number #$j" )

   $j +=1                          #It is equivalent to $j=j+1

end
```

The above code generates the following output:

This is the statement number 1

This is the statement number 2

This is the statement number 3

This is the statement number 4

The *while* modifier

Syntax of the while modifier is as follows:

block of code while condition

OR

begin

 block of code

end while conditional

Here, the block of code is executed repeatedly as long as the conditional evaluates to true. If the *while* modifier is specified after the *begin* statement, without providing the ensure clause or the *rescue* clause, the control executes the block of *code* one time, even before evaluating the conditional.

Example

```
#!/usr/bin/ruby

$j = 1

$n = 5

begin

  puts("This is the statement  number #$j" )

  $j +=1

end while $j < $n
```

The above code generates the following output:

This is the statement number 1

This is the statement number 2

This is the statement number 3

This is the statement number 4

The *until* Statement

The until statement can be thought of as the opposite of the while statement. If the until statement is used, the block of code is executed repeatedly as long as the conditional evaluates to false. Just like in the while statement, the reserved word 'do' separates the conditional and the block of code. A semicolon can also be used to separate them

until conditional [do]

   block of code

end

The following example illustrates how an until statement is used:

```ruby
#!/usr/bin/ruby

$j = 1

$n = 5

until $j > $n  do

   puts("This is the statement number #$j" )

   $j +=1;

end
```

The above code generates the following output:

This is the statement number 1

This is the statement number 2

This is the statement number 3

This is the statement number 4

This is the statement number 5

The *until* modifier

The syntax of the until modifier is as follows:

block of code until conditional

OR

begin

   block of code

end until conditional

The until modifier also executes a block of statement as long as the conditional evaluates to false. But, if the *until* modifier is specified after the *begin* statement, without providing the ensure clause or the *rescue* clause, the control executes the block of *code* one time, even before evaluating the conditional.

The following example illustrates how an until modifier is used:

```
#!/usr/bin/ruby

$j = 1

$n = 5

begin
```

```
puts("This is the statement number #$j" )

 $j +=1;

end until $j > $n
```

The above code generates the following output:

This is the statement number 1

This is the statement number 2

This is the statement number 3

This is the statement number 4

This is the statement number 5

The *for* statement

The for statement executes the block of code for all the number of elements specified in the range or expression.

Syntax of the' *for*' statement is as follows:

```
for variable [, variable ...] in expression [do]

   block of code

end
```

The following example illustrates how a for statement is used:

```
#!/usr/bin/ruby

for j in 1..6

  puts "This is the statement number #{j}"
```

end

In the above code, the range is given as 1..6, which means the puts statement is executed for every element from 1 to 6(including 6). The output generated is as follows:

This is the statement number 1

This is the statement number 2

This is the statement number 3

This is the statement number 4

This is the statement number 5

This is the statement number 6

If you use the *for* loop, a new scope is not created for the local variables. The reserved word 'do' separates the expression and the block of code. A semicolon or a newline character can also be used to separate them.

The loop can also be declared as follows:

```
#!/usr/bin/ruby

(1..6).each do |j|

  puts "This is the statement number #{j}"

end
```

The above code generates the following output:

This is the statement number 1

This is the statement number 2

This is the statement number 3

This is the statement number 4

This is the statement number 5

This is the statement number 6

The *break* Statement

The break statement is used to terminate a loop at any point. If a break statement is encountered, the control jumps out of the loop and is passed on to the statement that comes after the 'for' block.

The syntax for the break statement is simple and is as follows:

break

The following example illustrates how a 'break' statement is used:

```
#!/usr/bin/ruby

for j in 1..8

  if j> 4 then

    break

  end

  puts "This is the statement number #{j}"

end
```

The above code generates the following result:

This is the statement number 1

This is the statement number 2

This is the statement number 3

This is the statement number 4

What happened in the above program is that a range of numbers from 1 to 8 is declared in the for loop. Then, an if...then statement is specified within the loop and the condition is given as if(j>4). So, the loop starts from the element 1 and proceeds till the element 4, executing the puts statement for every iteration, till the element 4. When the element becomes 5, the if statement evaluates to true, passing the control to the break statement specified in the if block. As soon as the break statement is encountered, the loop terminates, leaving the elements from 5 to 8 unprinted.

The *next* statement

The next statement keeps on passing the control to the next iteration without executing the required block of code, as long as a condition evaluates to true.

It's syntax is as follows:

next

The following example gives you a clear idea about the functionality of the 'next' statement :

```
#!/usr/bin/ruby

for j in 1..8
```

```
if j < 4 then

  next

end

puts "This is the statement number #{j}"

end
```

Observe the output produced for the above code:

This is the statement number 4

This is the statement number 5

This is the statement number 6

This is the statement number 7

This is the statement number 8

What happened in the above example is that, as long as the if..then condition was true, the control was passed over to the 'next' statement. As soon as the 'next' statement is encountered, the control is passed over to the next iteration. The next statement keeps on handing over the control to the subsequent iterations without executing the puts statement, as long as the condition evaluates to true.

The *redo* statement

The 'redo' statement is used to restart an iteration, irrespective of the condition given in the for loop.

It syntax is as follows:

redo

The following example gives you a better idea of the functionality of the redo statement:

```
#!/usr/bin/ruby
for j in 1..8
  if j < 2 then
    puts "This is the statement number #{j}"
    redo
  end
end
```

The above code generates the following output, in which the statement goes into an infinite loop.

This is the statement number 1

This is the statement number 1

This is the statement number 1

. . . .

What happened in the above program is that, the redo statement in specified after the puts statement. So after executing the puts statement, the redo statement in encountered every time. As soon as the redo statement executed, the control is passed over to the start, restarting the loop beginning from the first element, which is 1 in this case. Since every time there is a restart of the loop, the puts statement goes into an infinite loop, repeatedly printing the statement pertaining to the element 1.

The *retry* statement

The retry statement in Ruby is similar to the redo statement, except that the retry statement is specified with the if ..then condition.

Its syntax is as follows:

retry

While using with the for loop, the syntax of the retry statement as follows:

for variable [, variable ...] in expression [do]

  retry if some_condition # restart from the first element of the expression

end

The following example gives you a better idea about the functionality of a retry statement:

```
#!/usr/bin/ruby

for j in 1..8

  retry if j> 3

  puts "This is the statement number #{j}"

end
```

The above code generates the following output, in which the statements for the first three elements go into an infinite loop.

This is the statement number 1

This is the statement number 2

This is the statement number 3

This is the statement number 1

This is the statement number 2

This is the statement number 3

This is the statement number 1

This is the statement number 2

This is the statement number 3

. . . .

Chapter 9:
Ruby Methods

Similar to the concept of functions found in a modern programming language, Ruby has the concept of 'methods'. By using methods, one or several statements exhibiting related functionalities are bundled together into a single unit.

Declaration and definition of methods

A lowercase letter should always be used as the beginning letter of the name of a method. If an uppercase letter is used as the beginning letter of a method's name, it will come off as a constant to the Ruby parser, making it parse an incorrect call.

If a method that has not been defined is called, an exception is raised by Ruby that an undefined method has been invoked.

The Syntax of declaring and defining a method is as follows

def method_name [([arg [= default]]...[, * arg [, &exp]])]

   expressions..

end

A simpler syntax can be given as follows:

def method_name

   expressions..

end

We can declare parameters of the method as follows:

def method_name (param1, param2)

  expressions..

end

Default parametric values, which have been preset, are passed if you call a method without providing the values of the required parameters:

def method_name (param1=value1, param2=value2)

  expressions..

end

If you want to simply call the method that does not require providing any parametric values, it is enough if you write the name of the method as follows:

method_name

On the other hand, if a method is to be called along with its parameters, the name of the method is written specifying the parametric values as shown below:

method_name 50, 35

You should be careful while passing parameters to a method, as if you pass the wrong number of parameters, an error is displayed by ruby. This is the drawback you may face if you use a method with parameters. For instance, for a method that requires four parameters, if only two parameters are passed, an error is displayed by Ruby.

The following example illustrates how a method is defined and called correctly:

```
#!/usr/bin/ruby

def testdata(a="Lizzy", b="Luke")

  puts "My first name is #{a}"

  puts "My last name is #{b}"

end

testdata "Jon", "Jasper"

testdata
```

The above code generates the following output:

My first name is Jon

My last name is Jasper

My first name is Lizzy

My last name is Luke

Return Values of a Method

By default, in Ruby, a value is returned by every method. It is last statement's value that is returned by the method. Consider the following example:

```
def testdata

  a = 1

  b = 10
```

```
c = 100
```

```
end
```

When the method *testdata* is called, the value of the last variable c is returned by the method.

The *return* statement

In Ruby, for a method to return a value(s), we use the return statement.

The syntax of the return statement is as follows:

return [exp[`,' exp...]]

If two or more expressions are specified, their values are returned as an array. If even one expression is not specified, the value *nil* is returned by the method.

The syntax of the return statement is as follows:

return

OR

return 20

OR

return 10,20,30

The following example illustrates the usage of the return statement:

#!/usr/bin/ruby

```ruby
def testdata

   a = 10

   b = 20

   c = 30

return a, b, c

end

var = testdata

puts var
```

The above program generates the following output:

10

20

30

Variable Number of Parameters

If a method is declared such that it accepts two parameters, those two parameters need to be passed mandatorily while calling the method.

But Ruby facilitates the declaration of a method such that variable number of parameters can be passed while calling the method. The following example illustrates how variable number of parameters can be passed to a method:

#!/usr/bin/ruby

```
def sampledata (*testdata)

  puts "The number of parameters is #{testdata.length}"

  for j in 0...testdata.length

    puts "The parameter is #{testdata[j]}"

  end

end

sampledata "Zachery", "16", "M"

sampledata "Maddison", "17", "F", "Dallas", "USA"
```

In the above example, a method named 'sampledata' is declared with a variable parameter named 'testdata'. We have specified the symbol * in front of the parameter, which means that the parameter can accept a variable number of values. So, the above code generates the following output:

The number of parameters is 3

The parameter is Zachery

The parameter is 16

The parameter is M

The number of parameters is 5

The parameters is Maddison

The parameters is 17

The parameters is F

The parameters is USA

Methods in a class

When you define a method externally to a class, by default, the method is set as *private*. If you define a method internally to a class, by default, the method is set as *public*. We can use *private* or *public* to change the method's default visibility.

You need an object for accessing a method that is declared and defined within a class. So, the class needs to be instantiated first, to facilitate the accessing of all the members of the class.

But, Ruby facilitates the accessing of methods from a class, without having to instantiate the class. The following example illustrates the declaration of a method in a class and how it can be accessed:

```
class SchoolLibrary

    def fee

    end

    def SchoolLibrary.return_date

    end

end
```

Observe the declaration of the method return_date. In the declaration, the class name is specified first, after which a period (.) follows. Then the method's name follows the period. This method can be accessed directly as shown below:

```
SchoolLibrary.return_date
```

No objects need to be created of the class SchoolLibrary, for accessing the method return_date.

The *alias* statement

We can use the alias statement for giving alternative names to global variables and methods. We cannot define an alias of a method, inside the body of the method. A method's current definition is retained by its alias, even if you override the method.

You cannot make aliases for the global variables that are numbered. For example, the global variables $1, $10, $100 etc; cannot possess aliases. Also, problems may arise if you override global variables that are built-in..

The syntax of the alias statement can be given as follows:

alias method_name method_name

alias global_variable_name global_variable_name

The following example illustrates how aliases can be created:

alias abc xyz

alias $amp $&

in the above lines of code, an alias 'abc' has been defined for the method 'xyz' and an alias $amp has been defined for $&.

The *undef* statement

This statement facilitates the cancellation of method's definition. We cannot use the *undef* statement inside the body of the method.

The alias and undef statements can be used for modifying class interfaces independently.

The syntax of the undef statement is as follows:

undef method-name

Example

For undefining a method named abc, we can use the undef statement as follows:

undef abc

Chapter 10:
How To Write A Web Application Using Ruby On Rails

Nearly everyone has heard of Ruby on Rails, even if you don't know what it is or what it means. For this chapter I am going to show you how to use Ruby on Rails to write a very simple web application just to show you how powerful Rails is and how fast it is at developing. I am going to tell you how to install the software you need, how to get started on a new project, how to manage the data, and much more, everything you need to get this application, and many more up and running.

Installing the Software

If you followed the first part of this book, you will already have the most up to date version of Ruby installed. If not, you need to refer back to my earlier chapter on how to install and set it up. Once you have done that, there are a couple of other pieces of software that you need to install:

Install Bundler gem

Bundler s a specific gem (package) that helps you to manage the dependencies needed when developing new projects. At your command prompt, type in

- gem install bundler

Next, you need to install Rails, the latest version so type in, at the command prompt:

- gem install rails -v4.2.3.rc2

The next step is to create the Rails app. When Rails is installed, it brings with it loads of libraries and command line tools and what we want to do now is install the skeleton of your new web app. Type this in to the command prompt:

- rails new bookmarks -T -d sqlite3 -B

Let me break down what you have just input:

Bookmarks - the name of your project

-T - Skip Test::Unit files. While this isn't really a fundamental part of the project, I have skipped them because testing is a subject for another time and would only complicate matters if I went in to them here.

-d sqlite3 - For this project, we are going to use SQLite database because it is the perfect fit for what we want. Rails supports a lot of different databases, even NoSQL databases so you will be spoilt for choice once you truly get going.

-B – this is saying that we do not want to run the bundle install because we will do it ourselves later on.

Once you have run that command, you should now see something like the following, which is explaining exactly what is going on:

- andrea@mbair ~/Works/12dos % rails new bookmarks -T -d sqlite3 -B

- create

- create README.rdoc

- create Rakefile

- create config.ru

- create .gitignore

- create Gemfile

- create app

- [...]

- andrea@mbair ~/Works/12dos % cd bookmarks

- andrea@mbair ~/Works/12dos/bookmarks %

You can see that a brand new directory has been created, called Bookmarks, which is the name of our project. Along with that, a whole bundle of files and directories has now appeared inside that directory.

Bundler and Gemfile – A First Look

You know that Bundler is a tool that helps you to manage dependencies within an app and it works by reading Gemfile which should be in the root directory of the app. Gemfile is required to ensure that all of the needed gems are installed properly including Rails itself, The following shows you what Gemfile is generated by the Rails ne command:

- source 'https://rubygems.org'

- # Our rails version

- gem 'rails', '4.0.0.rc2'

- # Use sqlite3 as the database for Active Record

- gem 'sqlite3'

- # Use SCSS for stylesheets

- gem 'sass-rails', '~> 4.0.0.rc2'

- # Use Uglifier as compressor for JavaScript assets

- gem 'uglifier', '>= 1.3.0'

- # Use CoffeeScript for .js.coffee assets and views

- gem 'coffee-rails', '~> 4.0.0

- # Uncomment this if you haven't a nodejs and coffeescript installed

- # gem 'therubyracer', platforms: :ruby

- [...]

What is happening here is that a default list of gems has been produced – these are the ones you need to begin working on your project. You will, throughout the course of your development, change this list, removing some and adding others.

Now you can run Bundle Install:

- andrea@mbair ~/Works/12dos/bookmarks % bundle install

- Fetching gem metadata from https://rubygems.org/..........

- Fetching gem metadata from https://rubygems.org/..

- Resolving dependencies...

- Using rake (10.0.4)

- Installing i18n (0.6.4)

- [...]

And that completes your bundle!

If you want to see where a specific bundled gem has been installed, use the command **'bundle show [gemname]** and you should see something like this:

- andrea@mbair ~/Works/12dos/bookmarks %

Run the Development Server

Although you haven't yet run any code, you are already able to use the default Rails development server so run this command:

- andrea@mbair ~/Works/12dos/bookmarks % rails server

  - ⇨ Booting WEBrick

  - ⇨ Rails 4.0.0.rc2 application starting in development on http://0.0.0.0:3000

  - ⇨ Run `rails server -h` for more startup options

  - ⇨ Ctrl-C to shutdown server

- [2013-06-14 16:10:48] INFO WEBrick 1.3.1

- [2013-06-14 16:10:48] INFO   ruby 1.9.3 (2012-04-20) [x86_64-darwin12.2.0]

- [2013-06-14 16:10:48] INFO WEBrick::HTTPServer#start: pid=1174 port=3000

- [...]

Now open up a browser and go to http://localhost:3000 and you will see the default welcome page.

An Introduction to MVC Patterns and Rails

Rails is defined as an MVC framework, which means that the behavior of the app is as such:

- **Model** – manages the data between the database and the rest of the application. You define how individual entities behave, including validation of data, before and after save hooks, etc., etc.

- **View** – This is the final output for a specific request and is normally HTML code, although it may be JSON or XML.

- **Controller** - The controller is, to all intents and purposes, the glue that holds the Model management and the Views together. Any http requests that come in to your application will be routed to the controller and that will then interact with at least one, maybe more, models to render the final output – the View.

Add a Bookmark Resource

The app we are building has a single goal – to manage bookmarks so the next step is to create the Bookmark resource:

- andrea@mbair ~/Works/12dos/bookmarks % rails generate scaffold bookmark title: string url:string

- invoke active_record

- create db/migrate/20130614142337_create_bookmarks.rb

- create   app/models/bookmark.rb

- invoke resource_route

- route   resources :bookmarks

- invoke scaffold_controller

- create   app/controllers/bookmarks_controller.rb

- [...]

On this occasion we have used a very useful command, Rails generate. We have built a scaffold that makes all of the files and the code that will automatically give you an MVC stack to manage the bookmark. Let's take a close look at what the command has done:

Database Migration

What we have done is specify that a bookmark records should consist of a title and a field called URL. Both of these are strings – default length of 255 characters. The rails scaffold generator has not created us a migration script so that your database schema can be updated:

- db/migrate/db/migrate/20130614142337_create_book marks.rb

- class CreateBookmarks < ActiveRecord::Migration

- def change

- create_table :bookmarks do |t|

- t.string :title

- t.string :url

- t.timestamps

- end

- end

- end

If you found this script easy to read, all well and good; if not, means:

- We have created a bookmarks table on a database

- The field Title and URL ae included and are of a string type

- We have also added in timestamps as default – these are translated automatically to **created_at** and **updated_at** date and time fields

But, at this stage, your database is not aware of the changes that have been made to the schema so you need to run the migration task:

- andrea@mbair ~/Works/12dos/bookmarks % rake db: migrate

- == CreateBookmarks: migrating
  =======================================

- create_table(:bookmarks)

- 0.0011s

- == CreateBookmarks: migrated (0.0012s)
  =======================================

Rake is another very useful and commonly used tool in the world of Ruby and it works similar to MakeFile in Ruby language. Rails includes a number of rake tasks that are ready for use but you can create your own custom ones if needed:

- andrea@mbair ~/Works/12dos/bookmarks % rake -T

- rake about   # List versions of all Rails frameworks and the environment

- rake assets:clean   # Remove old compiled assets

- rake assets:clobber   # Remove compiled assets

- rake assets:environment   # Load asset compile environment

- [...]

The Bookmark Model

The model that is used to represent a bookmark was created within **app/models/bookmark.rb.** Right now, it is virtually empty of code but it does know how it is meant to behave with the database. The following is a demonstration of that, using another common Rails command for opening a console:

- andrea@mbair ~/Works/12dos/bookmarks % rails console

- Loading development environment (Rails 4.0.0.rc2)

- >

Now we have created a shell that we can use to issue commands to our Rails app. Let's have a look and see if it knows anything about our Bookmark:

- Bookmark

- Bookmark(id: integer, title: string, url: string, user_id: integer, created_at: datetime, updated_at: datetime)

- Bookmark.count

- (0.3ms) SELECT COUNT(*) FROM "bookmarks"

- 0

It does know something about the bookmarks table, the fields contained within and how to query the database. So let's create a bookmark:

- Bookmark.create(title: "Hello Bookmarks app!", url: "http://localhost:3000")

- (0.1ms) begin transaction

- SQL (7.7ms) INSERT INTO "bookmarks" ("created_at", "title", "updated_at", "url") VALUES (?, ?, ?, ?) [["created_at", Fri, 14 Jun 2013 15:16:17 UTC +00:00], ["title", "Hello Bookmarks app!"], ["updated_at", Fri, 14 Jun 2013 15:16:17 UTC +00:00], ["url", "http://localhost:3000"]]

- (0.8ms) commit transaction

- #<Bookmark id: 1, title: "Hello Bookmarks app!", url: "http://localhost:3000", user_id: nil, created_at: "2013-06-14 15:16:17", updated_at: "2013-06-14 15:16:17

- Bookmark.count

- (0.3ms) SELECT COUNT(*) FROM "bookmarks"

- 1

The Bookmarks Controller and Views

So, earlier we said that the scaffold generator gave us all the MC stack parts so now it's time for the controller. Take a look in **app/controllers/bookmarks_controller.rb** and you should see a BookmarksController class and several methods. These are known as actions and each one corresponds to an HTTP path.

Routes

The last part of the MVC stack is all about routing the HTTP requests to the correct controller and action. To do this, the

Rails generator has made a change to **config/routes.rb.** A new line has been added – **resources: bookmarks** and this is the shorthand version of a command that tells it to use REST routes for the resource bookmark. If you want to know which routes are available, use the relative rake task, as such:

- andrea@mbair ~/Works/12dos/bookmarks % rake routes

- Prefix Verb   URI Pattern   Controller#Action

- bookmarks GET   /bookmarks(.:format) bookmarks#index

- POST /bookmarks(.:format)   bookmarks#create

- new_bookmark GET   /bookmarks/new(.:format) bookmarks#new

- edit_bookmark GET   /bookmarks/:id/edit(.:format) bookmarks#edit

- bookmark GET   /bookmarks/:id(.:format) bookmarks#show

- PATCH /bookmarks/:id(.:format) bookmarks#update

- PUT   /bookmarks/:id(.:format)   bookmarks#update

- DELETE /bookmarks/:id(.:format) bookmarks#destroy

Try the Server

Now we come to the fun bit. Start up the Rails server again and, using your browser got to http://localhost:3000/bookmarks/ - provided you have followed everything correctly so far you should now see the bookmark that you made earlier. If you don't, you can always click on the New Bookmarks link and create another one.

Now try http://localhost:3000/bokkmarks.json and see what happens. Although you have yet to write any code, you can see that this already does loads of things!

Adding Users and Authentication

Now that we have the bookmark resource, we need to have some Users that have bookmarks and we need a way of authenticating them. The Ruby and Rails community is hugely active and, no matter what your task is, there's no doubt that you will find a gem to help you. User authentication is one of the most common and there are a number of options. The most common is Devise so let's have a look at it.

First, you need to install the Devise gem so open up Gemfile and add in this lie:

- gem 'devise', '~> 3.0.0.rc'

We have also told bundler here that we want to use a version of Devise that is **greater_or_equal** to its minor version. Now run bundle install to install the gem

- andrea@mbair ~/Works/12dos/bookmarks % bundle install

- Resolving dependencies...

- Using rake (10.0.4)

- [...]

- Installing devise (3.0.0.rc)

- [...]

- Your bundle is complete!

To see where a bundled gem has been installed use 'bundle show [gemname]'

The output will look something like this

- andrea@mbair ~/Works/12dos/bookmarks %

And now you can run the Devise generator:

- andrea@mbair ~/Works/12dos/bookmarks % rails generate devise:install

- create config/initializers/devise.rb

- create config/locales/devise.en.yml

- =====================================
=====================================

If you haven't done this already, there is a little manual set up that you need to do:

1. Make sure that your environments files contain defined default URL options. An example of **default_url_options** that are suitable for a development environments in **config/environments/development.rb:**

- config.action_mailer.default_url_options = { :host => 'localhost:3000' }

Make sure that, in production, :host is set to your application's host.

2. Make sure that the definition of **root_url** s set to ***something*** in the **config/routes.rb file.** An example

- root :to => "home#index"

3. Make sure that you have got flash messages in **app/views/layouts/application.html.erb.**

3. Ensure you have flash messages in app/views/layouts/application.html.erb.

For example:

- \<p class="notice"\>\<%= notice %\>\</p\>

- \<p class="alert"\>\<%= alert %\>\</p\>

4. If you are using Rails 3.1 or higher on Heroku, set the following:

- config.assets.initialize_on_precompile = false

5. If you want to, you can copy Device views to your app. Do this:

- rails g devise:views

- ====================================
  ====================================

- andrea@mbair ~/Works/12dos/bookmarks %

This has resulted in two more files being created under **config/ directory:**

- **config/initializers/devise.rb -** this is where you can change Devise settings but, for the purposes of this tutorial, we are going to stay with the defaults.

- **Config/locales/devise.en.yml** – this is the default path for all rails app locales and it contains i18n translations for Devise.

Devise has also told us that we need to check five steps before we can complete the setup:

1. Open **config/environments/development.rb** ad add **config.action_mailer_default_url_options = {:host=> 'localhost:3000'}**

2. Go to **config/routes.rb** and define a root_url. For the purposes of this you can point **BookmarksController#index** to the root of the website**:**

- Bookmarks::Application.routes.draw do # [...] root 'bookmarks#index'

- # [...] end

3. Open **app/views/layouts/application.html.**erb ad add in the two bits of HTML code. This file will be the main app layout.

4. You can skip this one because you are, or should be, running the latest version of Rails

5. Use the command **rails generate devise:views** to generate the default views. These have a scaffold in them to make Devise work. If you see loads of generated views, please do not panic – we are only going to use a small section of them for now.

Generate a User Model

So, that is Devise set up but we still need to create a user model:

- andrea@mbair ~/Works/12dos/bookmarks % rails generate devise User

- invoke active_record

- create db/migrate/20130617132545_devise_create_users.rb

- create app/models/user.rb

- insert app/models/user.rb

- route devise_for :users

When we generated the Bookmark, we used a scaffold generator. This is a similar one but is focused only on the model and the route that informs Devise how it should handle **/uses/*paths**. Edit the whole sequence so it looks like this:

- class DeviseCreateUsers < ActiveRecord::Migration

- def change

- create_table(:users) do |t|

- ## Database authenticatable

- t.string :email,   :null => false, :default => ""

- t.string :encrypted_password, :null => false, :default => ""

- ## Rememberable

- t.datetime :remember_created_at

- t.timestamps

- end

- add_index :users, :email,   :unique => true

- end

- end

Also, the model needs to reflect the changes made to the migration:

- class User < ActiveRecord::Base

- devise :database_authenticatable, :registerable,

- :rememberable, :validatable

- end

Finally, you can use command **rake db:migrate** to run it.

What we have now is a very simple system that allows a user to register with the website, login and log out again. If you try running rake routes, you will see that there are now new routes for all of these actions and each one is referred to users.

Users and Bookmarks

Now we have both a User and a Bookmark, it's time to associate them. In this case, we are associating one to many. We now need to create a new migration, as such:

- rails generate migration AddUserIdToBookmark user_id:integer

Try to choose an appropriate name; it isn't required for this tutorial but it is a habit you should get into. The newly generated migrations adds a **user_id** integer column into the Bookmarks table.

Right now, neither of the two Rails models have any knowledge of one another. All we have done is put another field in the database but, without a few extra instructions, it's all pretty meaningless. What you need to do is this:

- add **has_many:bookmarks** into app/models/user.rb

- Add **belongs_to:user** to app/models/user.rb

These changes will associate a User instance with a bookmarks method and all of the records with that specific user ID will be referred to it,

Require Authentication for Bookmark Management

Now, if we take a look at the models, it looks as if the data part is all working. But, the BookmarksController that was created by the scaffold command doesn't yet apply any kind of authentication check so it needs a bit of work. First, you must check the user authentication before any action can be executed:

- class BookmarksController < ApplicationController

- # other before_actions

- before_action :authenticate_user!

- # [...] actions

- end

From here on in, any request that arrives on the BookmarksController will first be checked for authentication and then redirected to the login page.

To access the bookmarks that are owned by the authenticated used, you must replace **Bookmark occurrencies** with **current_user.bookmarks.** Current_user is the Devise object that is representative of the authenticated user while **.bookmarks** is the method that is provided by the model association between the Bookmark and User models.

Try the Server

If you haven't played around with this yet, try it now. First point your browser to http://localhost:3000 and it should automatically redirect you to the users/sign_in page. If you haven't yet registered a user, go to http://localhost:3000/users/sign_up and register one.

Handling Wrong Inputs

We do have a number of ideas as to where incorrect user input could cause damage to your application:

- If they provide incomplete data or wrong data when they create a new bookmark

- If they request an id for a bookmark that is non-existent which will cause an ugly error to form in your app

Let's take a closer look at how to deal with these issues.

Model Validations

If you attempt to use a password that is not long enough, i.e. shorter than 8 characters, or a wrongly formatted email during registration, Devise will pick up those errors and will not save the record. This will render the user registration form for another go. To put some validations in your app on the Bookmark model, change **app/models/bookmark.rb** as such:

- class Bookmark < ActiveRecord::Base

- belongs to :user

- # ensure that a user_id is present

- validates :user_id, presence: true

- # ensure that title is present and at least 10 chars long

- validates :title, length: { minimum: 10 }, presence: true

- # ensure the url is present, and respects the URL format for http/https

- validates :url, format: {with: Regexp.new(URI::regexp(%w(http https)))}, presence: true

- end

These validations should be pretty much self-explanatory.

When Resources are not Found

The second issue we mentioned was about trying to use an id that doesn't exist. There are a few ways to handle this but the easiest way is to redirect the index using a flash message. To do this, we need to change some code in the BookmarksController:

- class BookmarksController < ApplicationController

- # [...] other code here

- private

- # Use callbacks to share common setup or constraints between actions.

- def set_bookmark

- unless @bookmark = current_user.bookmarks.where(id: params[:id]).first

- flash[:alert] = 'Bookmark not found.'

- redirect_to root_url

- end

- end

- end

Set_bookmark is a method that is called **before_action** but only for those actions that require a resource id, such as update, show, destroy and edit. The new code lines will check for database existence and, if the id is not there, the user will then be redirected to the root path with a flash message.

Making Improvements a Step at a Time

Your app is almost finished but it is still lacking in a number of details that make a huge difference so let's start with the first one:

- **Add a good root page**

This is a pretty simple task and all we need is to create a new route, controller and view. This time though, we will use a controller dedicated generator.

- rails generate controller site index

For now, I have not put the output in because, by now, you should be able to guess what the result will be. A new SiteController has been created with a new action called index and there is a related view in **apps/views/site/index.html.erb** along with a new route in **config/routes.rb.** That said, the route needs to be changed to reflect what we want to achieve:

- Bookmarks::Application.routes.draw

- # [...] other routes

- # Comment/remove these lines

- # get "site/index"

- # root 'bookmarks#index'

- # Use this

- root 'site#index'

- end

Try loading http://localhost:3000 now and all you will get is an empty template for apps/views/site/index.html.erb. In order to render the content we must change the controller in app/controllers/site_controller.rb:

- class SiteController < ApplicationController

- def index

- # retrieve all Bookmarks ordered by descending creation timestamp

- @bookmarks = Bookmark.order('created_at desc')

- end

- end

While in apps/views/site/index.html.erb, you might see this as a starting point:

- <h2>Latest Bookmarks</h2>

- <table style="width: 100%">

- <thead>

- <tr>

- `<th>Url</th>`

- `</tr>`

- `</thead>`

- `<tbody>`

- `<% @bookmarks.each do |bookmark| %>`

- `<tr>`

- `<td><%= link_to bookmark.title, bookmark.url %></td>`

- `</tr>`

- `<% end %>`

- `</tbody>`

- `</table>`

Again, see the controller has processed the request by getting some records from the database by going through Bookmark, and then rendering the view that has the correct data in it.

Nicer GUI

If you want to pretty up your design and site layout, there are a number of css frameworks that can help you. You could choose the standard Twitter Bootstrap one but, for this, I have chosen something a little more fancy, called ZURB Foundation. Luckily, there is a gem for ZURB so we can integrate it into our rails app:

- `gem 'zurb-foundation', '~> 4.2.2'`

116

Now you can run the bundle install and the install generator:

- rails generate foundation:install

Once you execute this command, you will be asked to overwrite the existing application layout in app/views/layouts/application.html.erb/ Just press Y.

You can also now get rid of the stylesheets in the old scaffold:

- rm app/assets/stylesheets/scaffolds.css.scss

Make Your Forms Look Prettier

There is no doubt that forms do look ugly and they are pretty boring to write but we can use another gem to change that. Add this to your gemfile:

- gem 'simple_form', '~> 3.0.0.rc'

Again, run the bundle install and the install generator

- rails generate simple_form:install --foundation

At the same time, we are going to regenerate Devise views because this supports the SimpleForm gem we just installed:

- rails generate devise:views

The generator will want to know if you intend to overwrite the existing files, just press Y

The final step is to fix the form for Bookmarks because this one wasn't updated by the other generators. We can use the following content in app/views/bookmarks/_form.html.erb:

- <%= simple_form_for(@bookmark) do |f| %>

- `<%= f.error_notification %>`

- `<div class="form-inputs">`

- `<%= f.input :title %>`

- `<%= f.input :url %>`

- `</div>`

- `<div class="form-actions">`

- `<%= f.button :submit %>`

- `</div>`

- `<% end %>`

Congratulations! You have reached the end of this tutorial and, if you followed it correctly, you should now have a working yet basic, Ruby on Rails app. This is really only the beginning there is so much more to Ruby on Rails but perhaps that is a subject best left for a more advanced chapter.

Chapter 11:
The Command Line in Rails

If you are planning to use Rails, it is important that you be well versed with a few commands of the command line. The commonly used commands are listed as follows, in the order of the frequency of their usage.

1. rails console

2. rails server

3. rake

4. rails generate

5. rails dbconsole

6. rails new app_name

We can use either −help or −h with all the commands, if we want more information to be listed.

You can better understand the commands and their functions if they are explained in the context of creating a simple Rails application as follows:

rails new

We need to first install Rails for creating a Rails application. After the installation, we use the command 'rails new command' for creating a new Rails application,.

If your system doesn't have rails gem, you need to install it through the command gem install rails

```
$ rails new commandsapp

    create

    create  README.rdoc

    create  Rakefile

    create  config.ru

    create  .gitignore

    create  Gemfile

    create  app

    . . . . . .

    create  tmp/cache

    . . . . . .

       run  bundle install
```

As you can see, so much stuff will be set up by Rails even though the command is such a small one. The Rails directory structure is set up in all its entirety, so that you have all the code required for running a simple Rails application.

rails server

WEBrick is a small web server that comes along with Ruby. You need to use the rails server command to launch the WEBrick server. This is so that your application can be accessed by you through the web server as many times as you want.

The Rails application is run by the *rails server* command as follows:

$ cd commandsapp

$ bin/rails server

=> Booting WEBrick

=> Rails 4.2.0 application starting in development on http://localhost:3000

=> Call with -d to detach

=> Ctrl-C to shutdown server

[2013-08-07 02:00:01] INFO WEBrick 1.3.1

[2013-08-07 02:00:01] INFO ruby 2.0.0 (2013-06-27) [x86_64-darwin11.2.0]

[2013-08-07 02:00:01]
INFO WEBrick::HTTPServer#start: pid=69680 port=3000

After using the three commands, the Rails server is ready to listen on the port number 3000. Open your browser and type the address http://localhost:3000. After the link is opened, you can see that the basic Rails app is being run.

Instead of using the name 'server', its alias 's' can also be used for starting the server. The command goes like this:

rails s.

if you want the server running on another port, you can use the -p option. You can use the -e option for changing the default development environment.

$ bin/rails server -e production -p 4000

Rails can be bound to the required IP by using the -b option. Rail is bound to the localhost by default. A server can be run as a daemon, if we use the -d option.

rails generate

So many things can be created using the command *rails generate*. This command makes use of templates for creating things. A list of all the generators available can be generated by using the *rails generate* command.

Instead of using the word 'generate', its alias 'g' can be used fro invoking the generator command. The alias can be used a sfollows:

 rails g.

$ bin/rails generate

Usage: rails generate GENERATOR [args] [options]

...

...

Please choose a generator below.

 Rails:

 assets

controller

generator

...

...

More generators can be installed using the generator gems and they can also be created on your own.

A code known as the boilerplate code is required for the working of the app. The generators write the boilerplate code, thereby saving a lot of time for the user.

We can use the controller generator for making a controller of our own. We can find out which command we need to use, by asking the generator.

Help text is present for all the utilities of the Rails console. We can add to the end either –h or –help, just like seen in the *nix utilities.

Example: rails server --help.

$ bin/rails generate controller

Usage: rails generate controller NAME [action action] [options]

...

...

Description:

...

The controller name can be specified as a path, for creating a controller within a module. The path can be given as follows:

'parent_module/controller_name'.

...

Example:

`rails generate controller CreditCards open debit credit close`

Credit card controller with URLs like /credit_cards/debit.

Controller: app/controllers/credit_cards_controller.rb

Test: test/controllers/credit_cards_controller_test.rb

Views: app/views/credit_cards/debit.html.erb [...]

Helper: app/helpers/credit_cards_helper.rb

Parameters are expected by the controller generator, in the generate controller form ControllerName action1 action2.

Now, let us create something nice. A Greetings controller can be made having **hello** as an action, that would say something nice to the user.

$ bin/rails generate controller Greetings hello

create app/controllers/greetings_controller.rb

route get "greetings/hello"

invoke erb

create   app/views/greetings

create   app/views/greetings/hello.html.erb

invoke test_unit

create   test/controllers/greetings_controller_test.rb

invoke helper

create   app/helpers/greetings_helper.rb

invoke assets

invoke   coffee

create   app/assets/javascripts/greetings.js.coffee

invoke   scss

create   app/assets/stylesheets/greetings.css.scss

What has been generated by all of the above? The list of things done by all of the above is as follows:

1.It ensured that our application has a bunch of directories in it.

2. A controller file was created

3.A functional test file and view file were also created

4. A view helper, a JavaScript and style sheet files were also created.

The controller can be modified a little after checking it out (in app/controllers/greetings_controller.rb):

```
class GreetingsController < ApplicationController

 def hello

  @message = "Hello, how are you today?"

 end

end
```

And comes the view for displaying our message (in app/views/greetings/hello.html.erb):

```
<h1>A Greeting for You!</h1>

<p><%= @message %></p>
```

The server can be fired up with the help of the rails server.

```
$ bin/rails server

=> Booting WEBrick...
```

The URL is as follows: http://localhost:3000/greetings/hello.

For normal Rails applications, the pattern followed by the URL is as follows: http://(host)/(controller)/(action),

Rails also make the generators be available for data models.

For keeping track of the highest video game score made by you, you will create 'HighScore', an uncomplicated resource.

$ bin/rails generate scaffold HighScore game:string score:integer

invoke active_record

create   db/migrate/20130717151933_create_high_scores.rb

create   app/models/high_score.rb

invoke   test_unit

create   test/models/high_score_test.rb

create   test/fixtures/high_scores.yml

invoke resource_route

 route   resources :high_scores

invoke scaffold_controller

create   app/controllers/high_scores_controller.rb

invoke   erb

create   app/views/high_scores

create   app/views/high_scores/index.html.erb

create   app/views/high_scores/edit.html.erb

create   app/views/high_scores/show.html.erb

create   app/views/high_scores/new.html.erb

```
    create    app/views/high_scores/_form.html.erb
    invoke    test_unit
    create    test/controllers/high_scores_controller_test.rb
    invoke    helper
    create    app/helpers/high_scores_helper.rb
    invoke    jbuilder
    create    app/views/high_scores/index.json.jbuilder
    create    app/views/high_scores/show.json.jbuilder
    invoke  assets
    invoke    coffee
    create    app/assets/javascripts/high_scores.js.coffee
    invoke    scss
    create    app/assets/stylesheets/high_scores.css.scss
    invoke  scss
  identical   app/assets/stylesheets/scaffolds.css.scss
$ bin/rake db:migrate

== CreateHighScores: migrating
==================================================

-- create_table(:high_scores)
```

```
   -> 0.0017s
```

```
==  CreateHighScores: migrated (0.0019s)
========================================
```

Let us see what unit tests are. We can perform unit testing by taking a unit of a code and testing it for input and output. Unit tests are a gift. The sooner you realize that unit testing makes life easier for you, the better it is. The unit can be a module or a program.

The following is the interface that rails creates for the

$ bin/rails server

Open your browser and type in the address http://localhost:3000/high_scores, if you want to create new high scores (56,275 on Space Invaders!)

rails console

The console command facilitates the interaction of the user with the application through the command line interface.

The console can be invoked using the alias "c" as follows: rails c.

The user can specify the environment where you want the runner command to run.

$ bin/rails console staging

For testing out a code without making any changes in the data, you need to invoke the rails console --sandbox.

$ bin/rails console --sandbox

Loading development environment in sandbox (Rails 4.2.0)

Any modifications you make will be rolled back on exit

irb(main):001:0>

The app and helper objects

The app and helper objects can be accessed from the rails console.The url and path helpers can be accessed by using the app method. Requests can also be made using the app method.

>> app.root_path

=> "/"

>> app.get _

Started GET "/" for 127.0.0.1 at 2014-06-19 10:41:57 - 0300

...

The helpers of the application and Rails can be accessed using the helper method as follows:

>> helper.time_ago_in_words 30.days.ago

=> "about 1 month"

>> helper.my_custom_helper

=> "my custom helper"

rails dbconsole

rails dbconsole does two things:

- It determines what database is being used by the user.

- It puts you in a command line interface that goes with the database you are using and also determines the required command line parameters.

The databases supported by this command are

MySQL

PostgreSQL

SQLite

SQLite3.

The dbconsole can be invoked by using the alias 'db' as follows: rails db.

rails runner

runner is used for the non-interactive running of the Ruby code. The code is run in the context of Rails. For instance:

$ bin/rails runner "Model.long_running_method"

The runner can be invoked by using the alias "r" as follows: rails r.

The -eswitch is used for specifying the environment where you want the runner command to run.

$ bin/rails runner -e staging

"Model.long_running_method"

rails destroy

Destroy and generate can be thought of as opposites.What *destroy* does is, it finds out and undoes whatever the generate did.

The destroy can also be invoked using its alias "d" as follows: rails d.

$ bin/rails generate model Oops

    invoke active_record

    create   db/migrate/20120528062523_create_oops.rb

    create   app/models/oops.rb

    invoke   test_unit

    create   test/models/oops_test.rb

    create   test/fixtures/oops.yml

$ bin/rails destroy model Oops

    invoke active_record

    remove   db/migrate/20120528062523_create_oops.rb

    remove   app/models/oops.rb

```
invoke    test_unit
remove    test/models/oops_test.rb
remove    test/fixtures/oops.yml
```

Chapter 12:
Important Programs in Ruby

A Ruby program for printing the reverse of a string

```
def rev(text)

 puts text.reverse

end

rev("Lizzy")
```

OUTPUT: yzziL

A Ruby program to find if a given string is a palindrome or not

```
def palin(text)

  if text.reverse == text

    puts "The given string #{text} is a palindrome"

  else

    puts "the given string #{text} is not a palindrome"

  end

end

palin("madam")
```

OUTPUT:

The given string madam is a palindrome

A Ruby program to generate the Fibonacci series

```
def fib(count)

  a=0

  b=1

  puts a

  puts b

  current_count=0

  while current_count < count-2

   puts c= a+b

   a=b

   b=c

   current_count+=1

  end

end

fib(10)
```

A Ruby program to find the factorial of a given number

```
def factorial(x)
```

```ruby
 puts 1.upto(x).inject('*')

end

factorial(5)
```

A Ruby program to find the second biggest number from array

```ruby
def second_big(collection)

 puts collection.sort[-2]

end

second_big([15,13,14,56,34,23,76,99,56,32])
```

OUTPUT: 76

Conclusion

I hope that I have been able to teach you something about Ruby and about Rails. Remember that this is by no means a comprehensive guide, it is just an introduction for those who little to no knowledge of Ruby or experience with programming. I have tried to keep things simple, although the nature off computer programming language does not lend itself to looking all that easy.

I hope that, now you have a bit of knowledge about Ruby and Ruby on Rails that you will continue with your learning and go on to a more advanced program. Remember that practice makes perfect and, if you get stuck or start getting frustrated, step back, take a breather and start again. Eventually you will figure things out. When you have completed this tutorial and you move on, do one thing – figure out your own code, why it does what it does and how it works. Too many people copy and paste code off the internet without truly understanding it and they never actually learn anything

Thank you for downloading my book; if you enjoyed it and found it useful, please consider leaving a review for me at Amazon.com.